KENT
NARROW GAUGE

Vic Mitchell and Keith Smith

MP Middleton Press

Cover pictures. Upper - The old order is represented by Sir Tom, *one of BICC's well kept Bagnall saddle tanks used at Belvedere and seen on 20th May 1967, near the end of its career. (P. Groom)*

Lower - Narrow gauge revival is portrayed by Bronhilde *at the lower terminus of the immaculate Bredgar & Wormshill Railway, a truly authentic recreation. (P. G.Barnes)*

Back - Authors Keith Smith (left) and Vic Mitchell squat beside no. 2 Northern Chief *at Hythe on 16th May 1999, prior to its departure with the 1.00pm book launch train for their* Romneyrail *album (P.G.Barnes)*

Published May 2000

ISBN 1 901706 45 1

© Middleton Press, 2000

Design Deborah Esher
Typesetting Barbara Mitchell

Published by
  Middleton Press
  Easebourne Lane
  Midhurst, West Sussex
  GU29 9AZ
Tel: 01730 813169
Fax: 01730 812601

Printed & bound by Biddles Ltd,
  Guildford and Kings Lynn

CONTENTS

INDEX TO PUBLIC STATIONS

I. Location of the railways featured in relation to the principle main lines. All maps have north at the top, unless otherwise shown. (D.H.Smith)

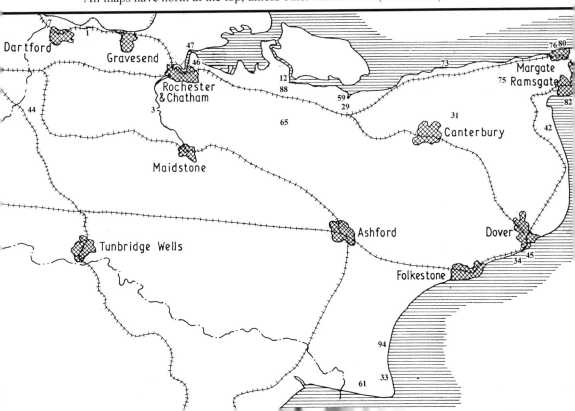

ACKNOWLEDGEMENTS

We are very grateful for the help received from so many of the photographers mentioned in the captions and also for assistance given by Dr D.Allenby (Edmund Nuttall Ltd), C.L.Caddy, P.Chappelle, D.Collyer, A.French, J.R.Fuller (SKLR), P.Hay, G.Holroyd, F.Hornby, S.C.Nash, A.Neale, J.S.Petley, Major F.P.O'Reilly (Lydd Ranges), G.T.V.Stacey and M.Turvey. The Eurotunnel diagrams appeared in the Proceedings of the Institution of Civil Engineers: *The Channel Tunnel Part I - Tunnels Special Issue 1992* and are reproduced by kind permission of T.J.Green and Thomas Telford Publishing. Our thanks also go to A.G.Nash who has trawled the Romney Hythe & Dymchurch Railway Association Archive so successfully for us, and our gratitude goes as ever to our usual helpers: G.Croughton, N.Langridge, Mr D.and Dr S.Salter and our wives.

INTRODUCTION

All the well known small gauge Kent lines are featured in this album, along with an extensive selection of less famous routes serving the diverse industries of the county; also included are some military establishments and a wide assortment of holiday locations. They have been chosen to represent the different uses to which light railways have been put over the last 100 years or more, in this interesting corner of England.

The classic *Industrial Railways of the South-East* (IRSE) contains illustrations of some lines not included herein, notably those of the Alpha Cement Company at Cliffe-at-Hoo, APCM at Northfleet, BSC at Rainham, Erith Loam Quarries, Lower Halston Brickworks, RPCM at Halling and the Swanscombe Cement Works. Colliery systems are also excluded.

Some of the military lines not featured in this volume were either short lived or subject to strict security. In the former category was a two-foot gauge construction railway on Manston Airfield for the RAF and in the latter was an Admiralty line on Hoo Ness and an Army network at No. 4 Storehouse RE, Ashford. There were many others.

Railways for leisure and pleasure have been remarkably numerous in the "Garden of England" and so only a representative selection can be offered. Again, some have been transitory. Some of the memorable ones being the Bridgehill & Beechwood Railway, the Folkestone Miniature Railway, Herne Bay Miniature Railway and the Saltwood Miniature Railway. We have only included one example of a line under 15ins gauge.

The terms "tramway" and "railway" were used loosely, especially on piers and even in the legal world, and so, in some cases, we have had to cross the blurred boundary.

While the Midlands had the Black Country, Dr. Edwin Course described parts of North Kent as once being known as the White Country, due to the impact of the unregulated cement industry. This area was once paradise for the student of industrial lines. Kent's geographical location and features made it a home for a diverse selection of military railways. Its coastline gave rise to many minor rail routes for the benefit of holiday visitors. We hope that you will enjoy our selection.

Vic Mitchell
Keith Smith
May 2000

1. Industry
APCM - STONE WORKS

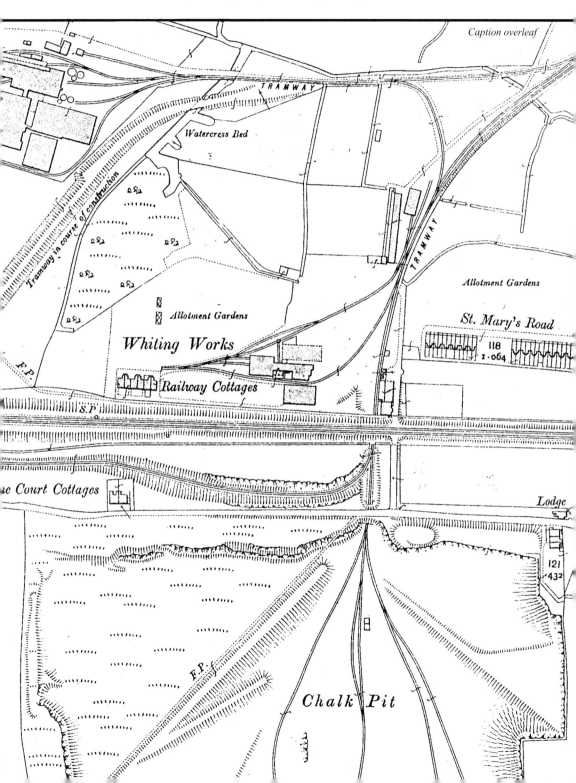

Caption overleaf

II. Associated Portland Cement Manufacturers Ltd was established in 1900 and it acquired all the cement works in Kent during the subsequent 50 years. It later became Blue Circle Industries. Its constituent businesses operated a large number of locomotives, most of which were standard gauge. Three of the narrow gauge systems are illustrated here. The unusual gauge of 3 ft 9½ins was employed at the works of I.C.Johnson & Co. Ltd, which was established on a site west of Greenhithe in 1877. The maps show the extent of their system in 1909, the one on this page being almost continuous with the one on the previous one. Both are at the scale of 20 ins to 1 mile.

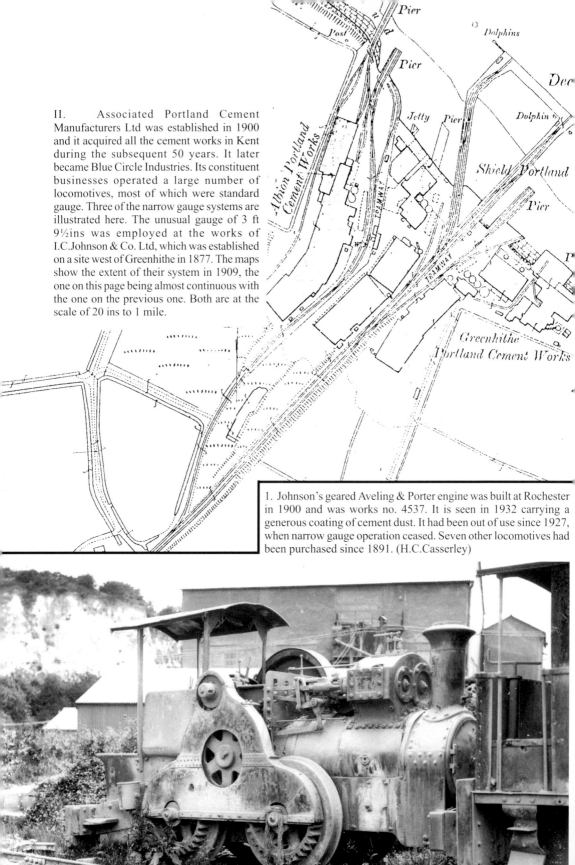

1. Johnson's geared Aveling & Porter engine was built at Rochester in 1900 and was works no. 4537. It is seen in 1932 carrying a generous coating of cement dust. It had been out of use since 1927, when narrow gauge operation ceased. Seven other locomotives had been purchased since 1891. (H.C.Casserley)

2. Johnson's 0-4-0ST *Leviathan* was built by Bagnall as no. 1609 in 1900 and was photographed on 2nd July 1932, when apparently in use as a static boiler. The replacement standard gauge system was much more extensive and can be seen on map V in our *Dartford to Sittingbourne* album. (H.C.Casserley)

APCM - HOLBOROUGH WORKS

III. The works was started in 1923 on a site north of Snodland, located between the A228 and the Medway Valley line of the Southern Railway. Some of the locomotives used on the standard gauge sidings can be seen in pictures 26-28 in our *Strood to Paddock Wood* album. A 1ft 11½ins gauge railway passed under this line and carried cement from the works to the wharves (see IRSE 35). The quarries were served by 3ft gauge systems, which are illustrated here. The first is shown west of Holborough on this 1940 map at 2ins to 1 mile. The second ran towards Paddlesworth.

3. This 0-4-0ST was one of only two steam locomotives bought for the quarry. It was Montreal works no. 54933 and was built in 1917. It arrived in 1928 and was scrapped in 1953. (J.H.Meredith)

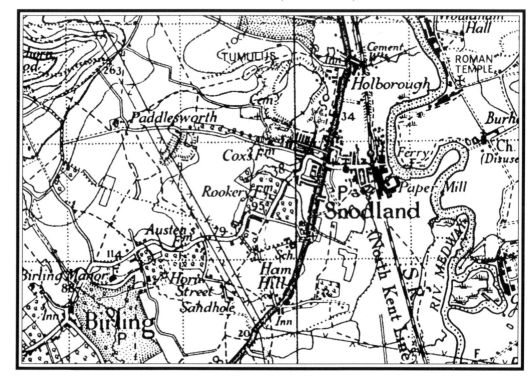

4. Ruston & Hornsby diesel no. 200524 was recorded on 8th August 1953 in the chalk quarry. The lines in this pit were relaid to standard gauge in 1954. The chalk passed under the main road in a pipe as a slurry. Also see IRSE 37 for sight of an 18-wagon train. (J.H.Meredith)

5. Clay was obtained from Paddlesworth pit, which was developed in 1952 and supplied with 3ft gauge track. The wagons were flat and carried tubs which were conveyed by aerial ropeway to the works. An inverted tub can be seen suspended near the centre of the picture. The locomotive is waiting to collect the empty wagons, as they gravitate towards the transfer shed.
(C.M.Jackson)

6. Some of the seven R&H diesels can be seen near the other end of the transfer shed in May 1967. The pit was closed in about 1969 and the equipment was auctioned in February 1972.
(C.M.Jackson)

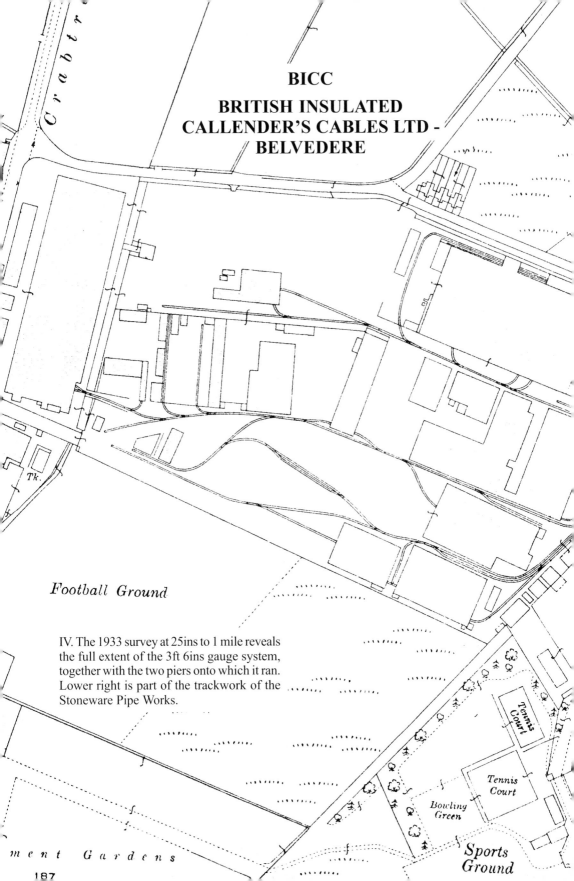

BICC

BRITISH INSULATED CALLENDER'S CABLES LTD - BELVEDERE

Football Ground

IV. The 1933 survey at 25ins to 1 mile reveals the full extent of the 3ft 6ins gauge system, together with the two piers onto which it ran. Lower right is part of the trackwork of the Stoneware Pipe Works.

Tennis Court

Tennis Court

Bowling Green

Sports Ground

m e n t   G a r d e n s

187

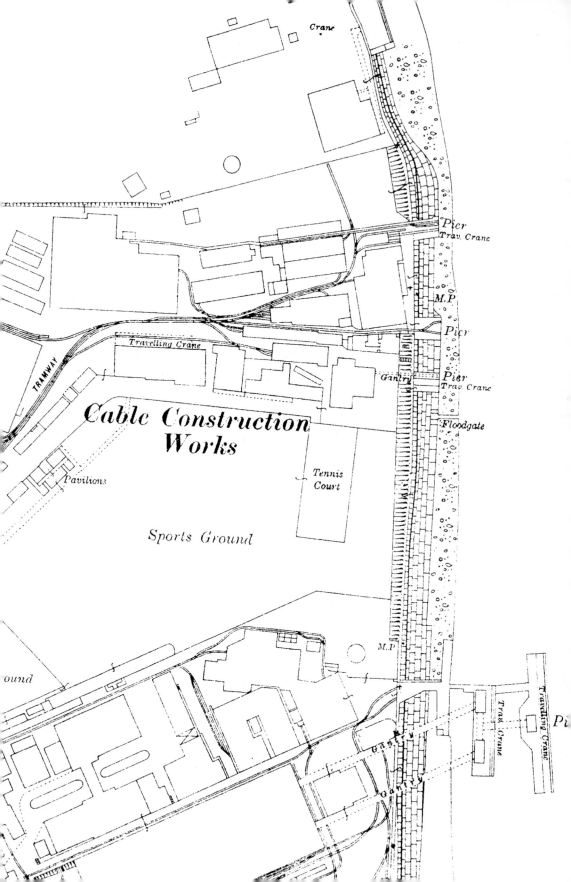

Crane

Pier
Trav. Crane

M.P.

Pier

Pier
Trav. Crane

Gantry

Floodgate

Travelling Crane

TRAMWAY

Cable Construction Works

Pavilions

Tennis Court

Sports Ground

M.P.

ound

Gantry

Gantry

Trav. Crane

Travelling Crane

Pi

7. *The Mighty Atom* was the unusual name given to one of three Bagnall 0-4-0STs on the site. The timber was used for making cable drums. Some more would be required for replacing the buffers. (J.H.Meredith)

8. Also photographed in August 1951 was Ruston & Hornsby diesel no. Y29, carrying a link of generous proportions. This was used between flat wagons when loaded longitudinally with large drums. Transverse seating was commonly employed on such locomotives owing to the frequent change of direction. (J.H.Meredith)

9. Seen in April 1959 is *Woto*, which had been built by Bagnall in 1924. All were converted to oil firing, hence the tank protruding from the far side of the cab. The locomotive is now privately owned and has been regauged to two-foot. It has been restored to coal firing. (H.C.Casserley)

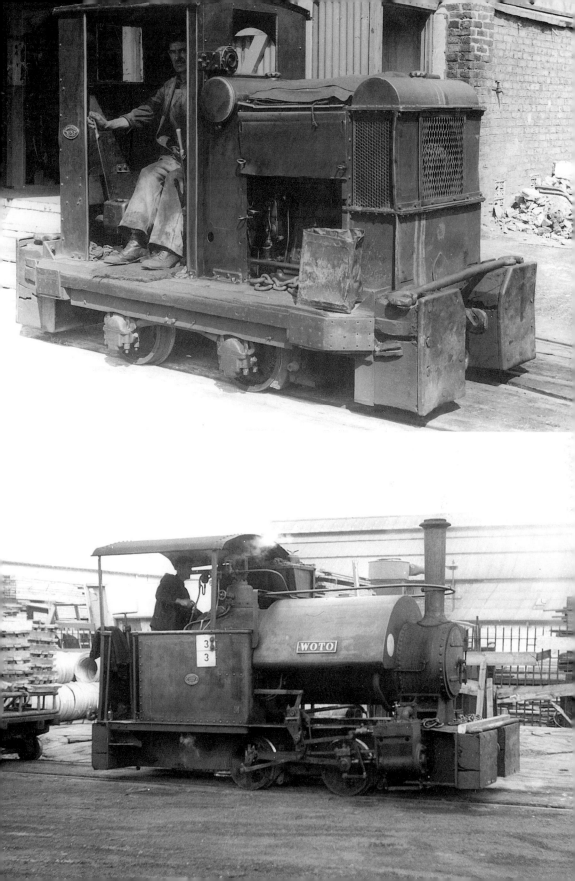

10. *Sir Tom* stands outside its shed on 11th March 1961. The steam locomotives outlasted the diesels; whether for mechanical or sentimental reasons is not recorded. The locomotive still exists in private ownership, although in many parts. (H.C.Casserley)

11. The other diesel, no. Y30, was recorded at work on the same day, shunting cable drums ready for refilling. The entire system closed in 1968. (H.C.Casserley)

BOWATERS - SITTINGBOURNE

V. In the days of small ships, the raw materials for paper making came up the Milton Creek (lower right) and only a short railway was required to the works. This was steam operated from 1908. Work began in 1913 on the construction of Ridham Dock, which could accommodate much larger vessels. A new paper mill was completed at Kemsley in 1924 and the track was extended to 10 miles (3½ route miles) to link all the sites shown on this Bowater map. The mills were owned by Edward Lloyds Ltd until 1948. Most of the locomotives are shown in alphabetical order in the following section, which illustrates the line before the southern part of the route was leased to the Locomotive Club of Great Britain (for a nominal sum) to operate from 1970. Map V in our *Branch Lines around Sheerness* shows the detail of Ridham Dock in 1939 and pictures 23 to 30 give other views of the railway.

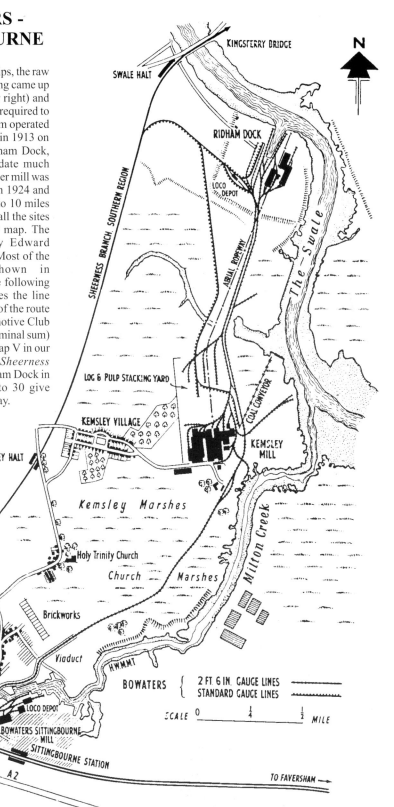

N

KINGSFERRY BRIDGE

SWALE HALT

RIDHAM DOCK

LOCO DEPOT

AERIAL ROPEWAY

The Swale

SHEERNESS BRANCH, SOUTHERN REGION

LOG & PULP STACKING YARD

COAL CONVEYOR

KEMSLEY VILLAGE

KEMSLEY MILL

KEMSLEY HALT

Kemsley Marshes

Holy Trinity Church

Church Marshes

Milton Creek

Brickworks

Viaduct

HWMMT

BOWATERS { 2 FT. 6 IN. GAUGE LINES ———
STANDARD GAUGE LINES ·········

SCALE 0 ¼ ½ MILE

LOCO DEPOT

BOWATERS SITTINGBOURNE MILL

SITTINGBOURNE STATION

← LONDON VIA CHATHAM

A2

TO FAVERSHAM →

12. *Alpha* was recorded on 16th May 1966 at Ridham Dock with the 12.25 staff train to Sittingbourne. Of 0-6-2T wheel arrangement, it was built by Bagnall in 1932 and remains on the line. With so much loose paper on the ground, a spark arrestor was an essential feature. (M.J.Messenger)

13. *Chevalier* was constructed in 1915 by Manning Wardle and was acquired from the Chattenden & Upnor Railway in 1950. It was photographed in fine condition in June 1957. (J.H.Aston)

14. *Chevalier* is included in this splendid panorama of Ridham Dock taken in May 1966, as bales of waste paper were being transferred from ship to rail. The locomotive was later sold to Whipsnade Zoo. (M.J.Messenger)

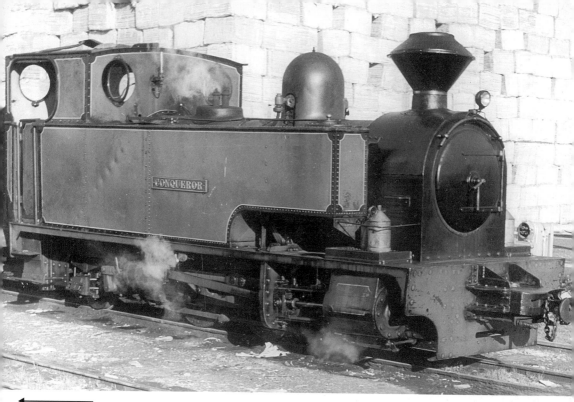

VI. The 1947 map at 6ins to 1 mile includes the southern part of the system, which is that part now preserved.

15. *Conqueror* was pictured on 15th October 1968, with bales as a background. The 0-6-2T was a Bagnall creation in 1922 and is now at Whipsnade Zoo. (J.H.Meredith)

16. *Excelsior* was photographed with a staff train on 14th May 1960. Until about that time, such trains had been composed of five coaches. The locomotive was built by Kerr Stuart in 1908 and also retired to Whipsnade Zoo. (R.C.Riley)

17. *Leader* stands outside the running shed at Sittingbourne on 30th July 1968. It was a Kerr Stuart product from 1905 and is still present on the railway. (P.Groom)

VII. The 1938 map at 25ins to 1 mile has the original railway running across the upper part and the later line to Kemsley Mill and Ridham Dock at the top. The present terminus is near the street named THE WALL.

18. *Melior* was purchased from Kerr Stuart in 1924 to shunt at Kemsley Mill. It remains as part of the fleet in use south thereof. The simple Hackworth valve gear was not widely used by other manufacturers. (P.Groom)

19. *Monarch* was unusual in having powered bogies (0-4-4-0T) and was sold in 1966 to become the Welshpool & Llanfair Railway's no 6. It had been built in 1953 by Bagnall. (M.J.Messenger)

20. *Premier* was photographed near the bale conveyor at Sittingbourne in August 1954. It was constructed by Kerr Stuart in 1905 and was one of the original trio. It remains, along with *Leader.* (H.C.Casserley)

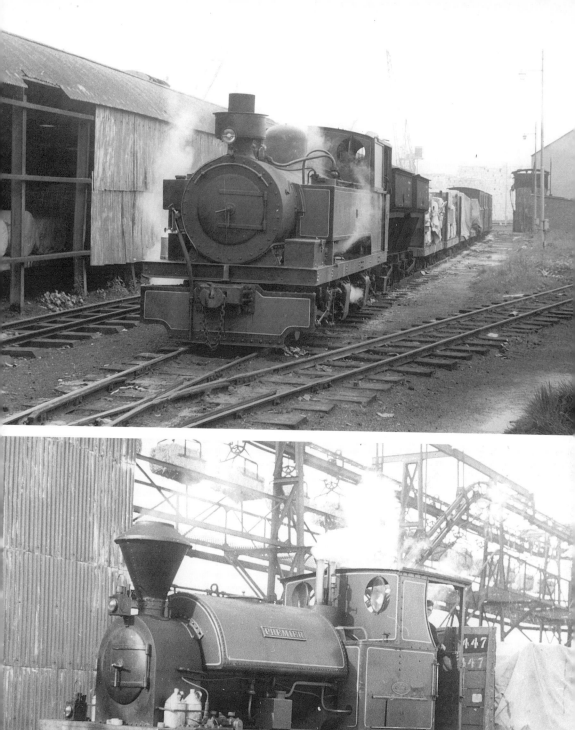

21. The pulp store at Ridham was a common habitat for *Superb*. The 0-6-2T is seen at work there on 3rd June 1964. (M.J.Messenger)

22. *Superb* dates from 1940 and was created by Bagnall. It is standing near the water tank and sand drier on 14th May 1960 and continues to grace Kemsley Marshes. (R.C.Riley)

23. *Superior* was an 0-6-2T obtained from Kerr Stuart in 1920. It is seen in October 1968, near the pulp wood stack at Kemsley, which was supplied by aerial ropeway from the dock. It is one of four now resident at Whipsnade Zoo. (J.H.Meredith)

24. *Triumph,* a 1934 Bagnall 0-6-2T, was used to haul the special train on 4th October 1969 on the occasion of the handover of the line to the LCGB, despite a slight technical problem. However, as the new road was not ready, the railway was used by Bowaters until 26th October 1969. (D.Trevor Rowe)

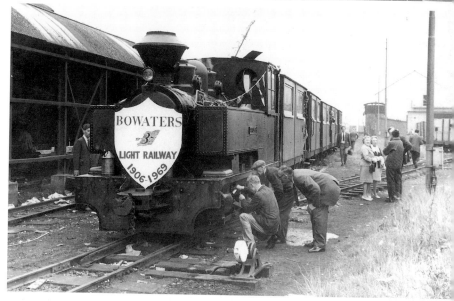

25. *Triumph* is on part of the half-mile long concrete viaduct across the marshes in August 1954. There is evidence of decay. There were 13 trains for workers during each period of 24 hours at that time. (R.M.Casserley)

26. The locomotive is now *Unique* in name and in fact, on this railway. Few narrow gauge fireless locomotives were made in any case. This example was built by Bagnall in 1924, for use in Kemsley Mill from where it was able to obtain steam intermittently. It is now a static exhibit at Kemsley Down. (P.Groom)

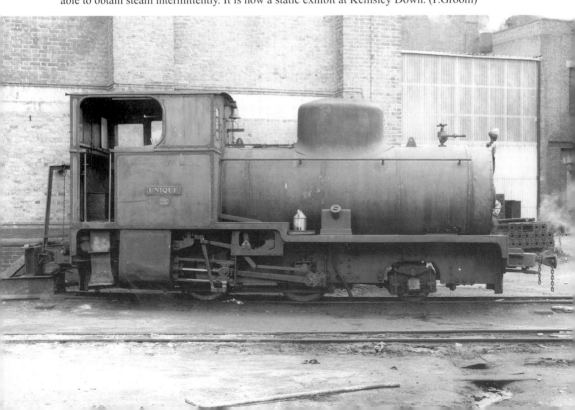

27. A Hudson-Hunslet diesel was obtained new from plant dealer John Heaver of Chichester, in 1953. It was a cancelled export order and was photographed in April 1966, but it was not popular and no other diesels were bought. It is still on the railway, carrying the name *Victor,* used on another fireless locomotive until it was scrapped in 1967. (P.Groom)

28. A battery powered locomotive was obtained from English Electric in 1921 and a shed was provided for it at Ridham Dock. It was cut up in June 1968. (P.Groom)

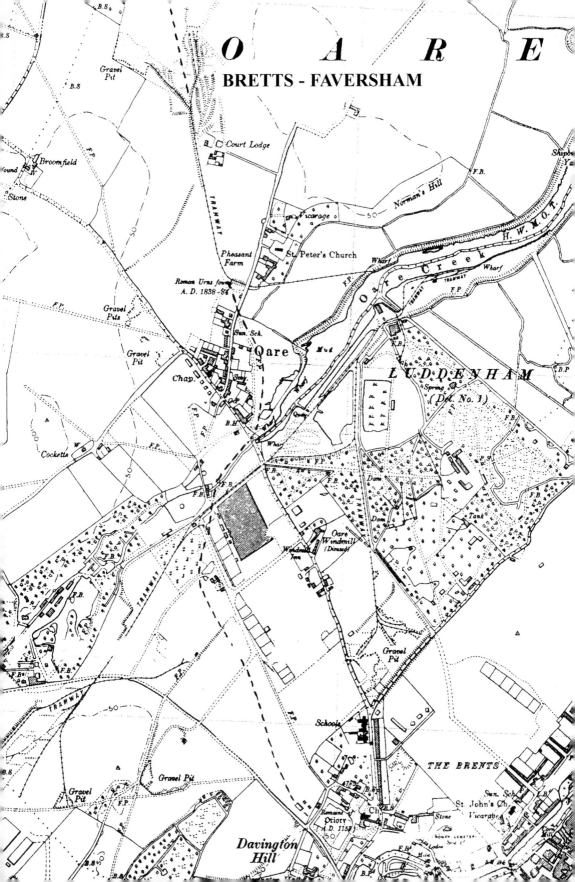

O A R E
BRETTS - FAVERSHAM

VIII. The 1938 survey, at 6ins to 1 mile, of the area north of Faversham includes two narrow gauge systems and also the end of the Faversham Creek branch of the SR, which is featured in our *Faversham to Dover* album. The lines south of Oare Creek were operated by the Ace Sand & Gravel Co. Ltd. and subsequently by Robert Brett & Sons Ltd. The dashes indicate the approximate route of the Davington Light Railway, described in caption nos. 59-60. It terminated on Uplees Marsh, just beyond the upper border of the map. The tunnel under the road, north of Oare, is still evident. Each terminus had two platform roads, separated by an engine release road. There was a passing loop near Oare Wharf, with an island platform for use by local workers.

29. Two photographs from 1968 show Brett's Motor Rail diesel with skip wagons. Drag-line excavators were well suited for use in gravel pits, but the loading of small skips required great skill, not evident here.(C.M.Jackson)

30. A thoughtless cyclist largely obscures the flagman, but not his straw hat. The high centre of gravity of these wagons, combined with indifferent track, resulted in many derailments. (C.M.Jackson)

BRETTS - STURRY

The pits were to the east of Sturry station and south of the main line. The pit north of the River Stour was worked first and a Bailey bridge was erected later over the River Stour, when the southern gravel pit was started.

31. Two Ruston & Hornsby diesels wait near the south pit in June 1967. The Brett-built skips were not of the crude tipper type, seen in the previous photograph, but they had a low centre of gravity and side doors. Rail operation ceased in about 1976. (C.M.Jackson)

32. Gravel delivered by road was conveyed to the primary washing pit in a tall bogie skip, hauled by a Simplex over a short length of track. Much of the mud or fines was removed at this stage. The overhead rail was for wagon stabilisation. (C.M.Jackson)

DUNGENESS: FISH RAILWAYS

33. The rounded pebbles of the Dungeness peninsular have made mobility of all types difficult. Walking has been made easier with ski-like attachments or boards, as seen in the foreground. By 2000, eight lines for the conveyance of fish remained, but only one was in regular use as concrete roads had increased in number. (N.Langridge)

EUROTUNNEL (TML)

IX. Track laying on the surface and construction of a rolling stock maintenance workshop had reached this stage by early 1988. Two adits were dug to running tunnel depth, A2 eventually having five narrow gauge tracks. The road tunnel from Upper Site is now open to the public for access to a nature reserve created on the spoil.

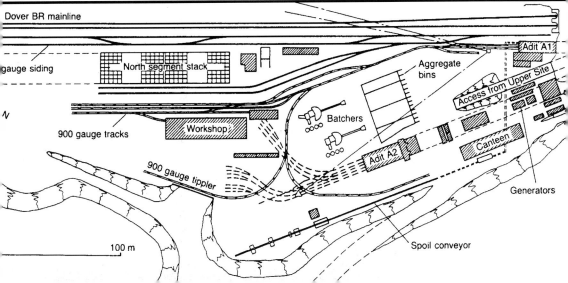

Transmanche Link (TML) was the consortium of firms set up to construct the tunnels and it created Underground Operations (UGO) to specifically construct, operate and remove a 3 ft (900mm) gauge railway system to serve the tunnellers during 1988-92. The facts have to be read slowly to appreciate their magnitude; this is by far the most important line in this book. We refer to the British part only; a similar operation took place on the French side. The work commenced on the site of a former colliery at the foot of Shakespeare Cliff, seen in pictures 95 to 99 in our *Ashford to Dover* album.

UGO employed 750 people, 78 electric locomotives, 66 diesels and 16 passenger trains. It removed material at the rate of up to 2400 tonnes *per hour* and ran up to 90 trains each way, each day, to each of the six tunnel boring machines, three landward and three seaward. Over 2.7 million tonnes of materials were taken into the tunnels, these including 1.6 million tonnes of lining segments and nearly 1.0 million tonnes of concrete. At one stage, grout was moved at the rate of 400 tonnes per day.

Each tunnel had double track, with many crossovers. Much single line working was necessary, owing to cross passage construction and fitting work obstructing one line. There was no signalling except at the adits, all train drivers being supervised by radio from a control room. The main routes and inclines had overhead electrification at 550 volts DC, but wires were not used. Instead, live and return conductors were formed of aluminium rods, coated with stainless steel. As the ventilation system developed, it was possible to use more diesel locomotives and ten electrics were thus converted in 1991.

Standard gauge track laying commenced near the middle of the seaward running tunnels and the service tunnel was provided with a roadway. Track in the landward tunnels was laid from the coast inland. Thus the railway had to convey all these materials in, and then remove all its own track between April 1991 and October 1992.

34. An eastward view from 3rd March 1989 includes six parallel tracks of the construction railway and part of the roof (right) of the rolling stock workshop. The lines converge at Adit A2, but only two had been laid therein by that date. A glimpse through the portal cranes reveals the stack of segments and also the train that had conveyed them from Grain. The segment factory, production and transport are illustrated in pictures 83 to 86 in *Branch Line to Allhallows*. (QA Photos)

35. This is the northern of two workshops in use during 1990 and is seen in February of that year. Slurry skips are nearest to us on the two wagon roads. The pair of electric locomotives on the right have batteries for working beyond the limits of overhead supply. (QA Photos)

X. The land area of Britain increased during the tunnel boring, the new coastline having first been outlined by two rows of sheet steel piles infilled with concrete. The spoil front and trackwork development in June 1990 are shown here. The desalination plant was necessary, as local water supplies were inadequate to meet construction requirements.

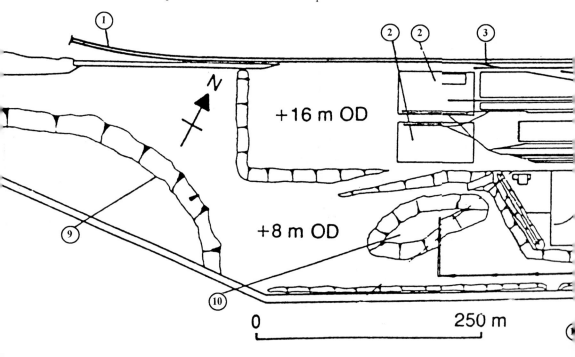

+16 m OD

+8 m OD

0   250 m

36. This is a close-up view of the area in the right background of picture no. 34 and was taken on 10th September 1991. It includes Adit A2, the harbour arm at Dover and one of the two pairs of Schoma 200hp electric locomotives forming the rescue trains. (R.C.Riley)

1.	London - Dover main line	10.	Temporary spoil stockpile
2.	Fixed equipment storage compounds	11.	General storage compounds
3.	British Rail access to standard gauge sidings	12.	Gantry cranes
4.	Segment stacks	13.	Spoil conveyor
5.	Concrete batchers	14.	Loco and rolling stock workshops
6.	Road access from upper site	15.	Entrance to rail adit A2
7.	Main substation	16.	Ventilation plant
8.	Conveyor adit A1	17.	Desalination plants
9.	Spoil front		

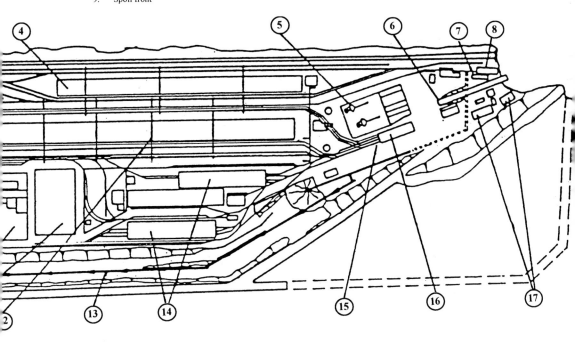

37. Quintuple track with rack operation is a rarity, especially with overhead twin conductors. These are protected by the inverted W troughs and terminate at the top of the 1 in 7 incline, battery power being used on the surface. Segments, each weighing up to nine tonnes, are about to descend, together with bagged cement. The outward bound locomotive on the left has just lowered its current collector arm on 6th February 1990. (QA Photos)

38. After descending the man-access shaft by double-deck lift from the top of Shakespeare Cliff, we would have emerged through a short tunnel on the right. It is obscured by the electrician. Only the drivers used the adit. The line straight ahead enters the landward service tunnel, while the track crossing it to the left becomes the centre rack railway in Adit A2. The photograph was taken early in 1990, as were the following three. (QA Photos)

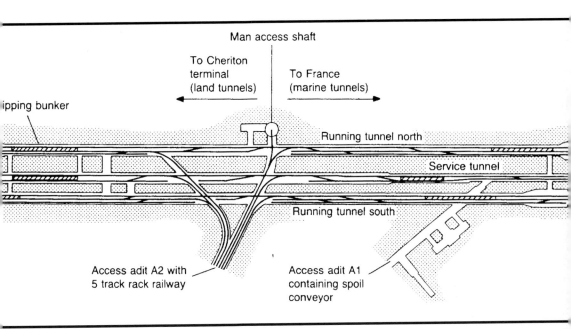

Man access shaft

To Cheriton terminal (land tunnels) ← | → To France (marine tunnels)

Tipping bunker

Running tunnel north

Service tunnel

Running tunnel south

Access adit A2 with 5 track rack railway

Access adit A1 containing spoil conveyor

XI. We now examine part of the underground system by looking at the complexity of the junctions between the land and marine tunnels. The six tipping bunkers are hatched; they discharged onto conveyor belts, which took the spoil to the surface via Adit A1; this crossed the route of Adit A2 underground.

39. Triple track with multiple crossovers was provided at the commencement of both marine running tunnels. There were 40 Hunslet/GMT Mk2 electric locomotives working in pairs, each providing 200hp. Their batteries were recharged from the overhead conductors, which can be seen exposed on the right. (QA Photos)

40. RS006 was one of 33 Schoma 185hp diesels and is seen in a service tunnel. Grouting trains caused much single line working, as did those involved in wiring and pipework. One of the air ducts is overhead. Rolling stock included 343 side tipping wagons, 611 flat and open wagons, 14 for cable drums, 11 for cement and 51 concrete remixer cars, known as "bullets". (QA Photos)

41. One of the 16 Schoma 80hp manriders is seen attached to a flat wagon and the ambulance, in one of the 25ft diameter running tunnels. Each two-car train carried 90 men. There were also 34 cars for inclusion in locomotive hauled trains and 31 mess/toilet cars. The railway transported about 10 million tonnes of muck and the train mileage was equivalent to circumnavigating the world each week or almost five return trips to the moon during the project! (QA Photos)

GUILFORD TRAMWAY - SANDWICH

XII. The exclusive St. George's Golf Club was founded in 1887, but it suffered from poor local transport. The same problem at a club near the Kent border was solved by the opening of the Rye & Camber Tramway in July 1895. Its engineer was H.F.Stephens (later Colonel) and he was invited to plan a similar line from Sandwich, but it was not adopted.

However, a freight-only line was eventually constructed from a wharf on the River Stour and a new locomotive arrived for it at the end of July 1903. The gauge chosen was 3ft 6ins, the same as the tramways of Thanet and Dover with which, it was optimistically thought, it might be joined.

The main traffic was building materials for the spacious mansions being built for the wealthy. Domestic coal may also have been conveyed. Owing to World War I, the line was little used after 1915, although in 1917-18 it occasionally served Army camps in the area. Their demolition in 1921-22 again involved steaming the locomotive, but it does not seem to have been used after 1930.

The route seems to have appeared only on a Geological Survey, in which Sandwich is in the shading on the left. The line commenced at Guilford Wharf, where there was a steam crane, a weighbridge, a loop and a locomotive shed. It ran past the golf clubhouse and a toll house, continued at the roadside and finally divided to run along both King's Avenue and Waldershare Avenue to the coast, where both turned northwards.

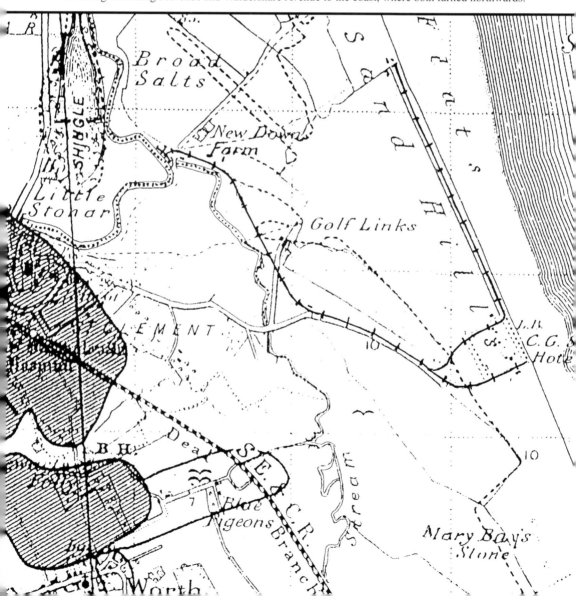

42. The tramway is in the foreground of this view of the seven-storey Guilford Hotel, which was opened in 1906 and was later rebuilt on a smaller scale. It was named after the Earl of Guilford, who was the local landowner. (Julian Arnoud coll.)

43. Waldershare Park was the Earl's home, hence the locomotive's name. It was ordered from Manning, Wardle & Company in May 1903 and was works no. 1611. It was photographed in 1912 and seems to have survived until about 1950. (I. Gotheridge coll.)

HEWITTS FARM - ORPINGTON

44. A 1½ mile long 2ft gauge line was laid in a roughly oval shape on a farm just north of Knockholt station during 1987. It provided transport on one of the biggest pick-your-own operations in Europe, but Bromley Council ruled that it was not permitted development on agricultural land. The train was photographed on 26th August 1990, immobilised and in use as a pickers' picnic parlour. The Baguley 0-4-0 diesel had been provided with three coaches. (D. Trevor Rowe)

NUTTALL'S DOVER SEWER

45. For almost two years, a 2ft gauge railway was in use during the construction of a one mile long tunnel, about ten feet in diameter, which was to serve as an interception sewer. It ran from a shaft in Farthingloe to Aycliff Fort, where this photograph was taken on 27th February 1998, one week after Edmund Nuttall Ltd had successfully completed the contract on time. Most of the heavy haulage had been undertaken by 12-tonne Hunslet diesels; one is being driven towards the tunnel's single track. A Clayton 4-tonne battery electric is on the right. (C.M.Jackson)

2. Military

CHATHAM DOCKYARD

The Dockyard was established in the reign of King Henry VIII, but it was not until the 1860s that the 18ins gauge internal railway system was begun. It was very extensive by the time that the survey overleaf was made in 1879. Standard gauge is shown from top to bottom of the left page. This line was laid after a branch from the LCDR was completed in 1877. (See *Dartford to Sittingbourne* pictures 89-98). Tracks of this gauge were gradually extended throughout the yard, often as dual gauge. The narrow gauge was little used after World War I and was abandoned in the 1930s. Initially horse worked, the first steam locomotive arrived in 1871 in the form of a Manning Wardle 0-4-0ST. There followed ten others of this wheel arrangement, six 0-4-2Ts and six 2-4-2Ts.

46. *Vulcan* was built by Vulcan Foundry in 1883 for the line, the other 0-4-2Ts coming secondhand from the Woolwich Arsenal system. Little remains of the fleet today, only a sectioned boiler.
(F.Jones/R.M.Lyne)

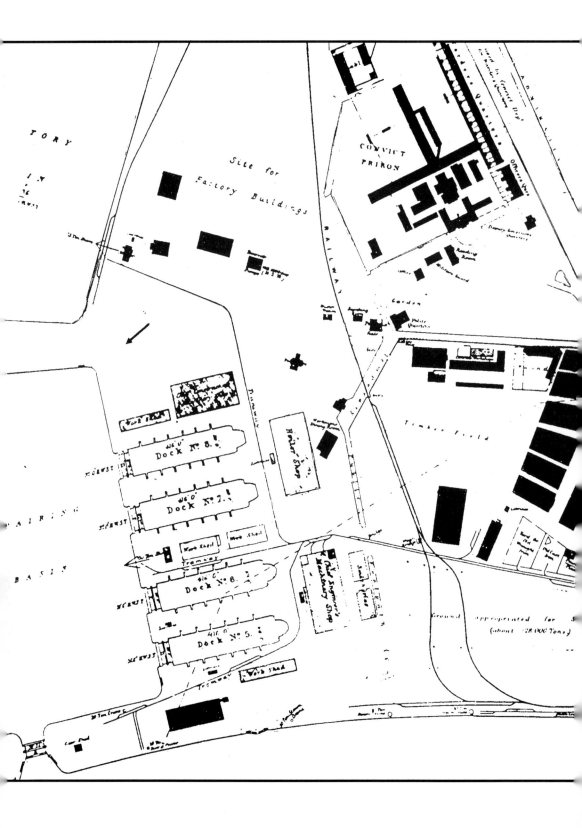

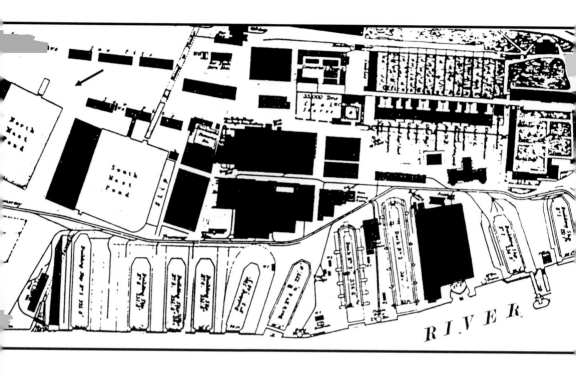

XIII. The Navy ceased to use the premises in 1984 and it was transformed into a massive and fascinating museum known as Chatham Historic Dockyard. It has been designated the World Naval Base since 1999. Much of the standard gauge track is still in place, but there is not much evidence of the 18ins gauge system. The upper right map continues from the left one and overlaps the lower one.

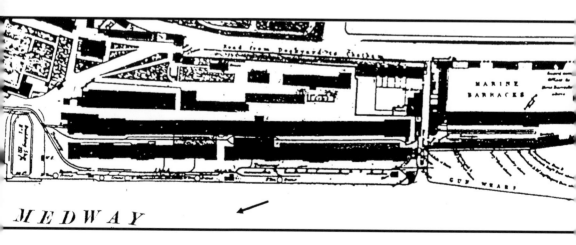

CHATTENDEN & UPNOR RAILWAY

XIV. The former SER branch to Port Victoria is described in our *Branch Line to Allhallows*. The lines from Sharnal Street to Lodge Hill and to Kingsnorth were also standard gauge, as was the first railway between Upnor and Chattenden. This was short lived and served an Army camp at the latter place during part of the 1870s. Its trackbed was used for a 2ft 6ins gauge line to serve the Royal Engineers training camp at Chattenden. Following its transfer to Longmoor, the railway passed to the Admiralty on 1st April 1906. It carried only Naval staff and a timetabled service was operated until 19th May 1961. It closed completely at the end of that year.

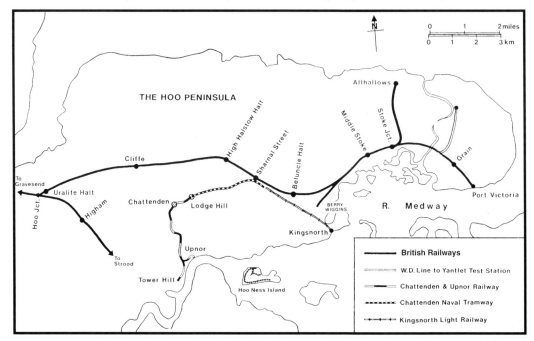

(R.M.Lyne)

LODGE HILL

47. The northern terminus was visited by the Railway Enthusiasts Club on 7th April 1956 and a special train was provided. Note the tall signal box, the weather vane above the semaphore signals and the fuel supply pipe, to the left of the Drewry diesel. (J.J.Smith)

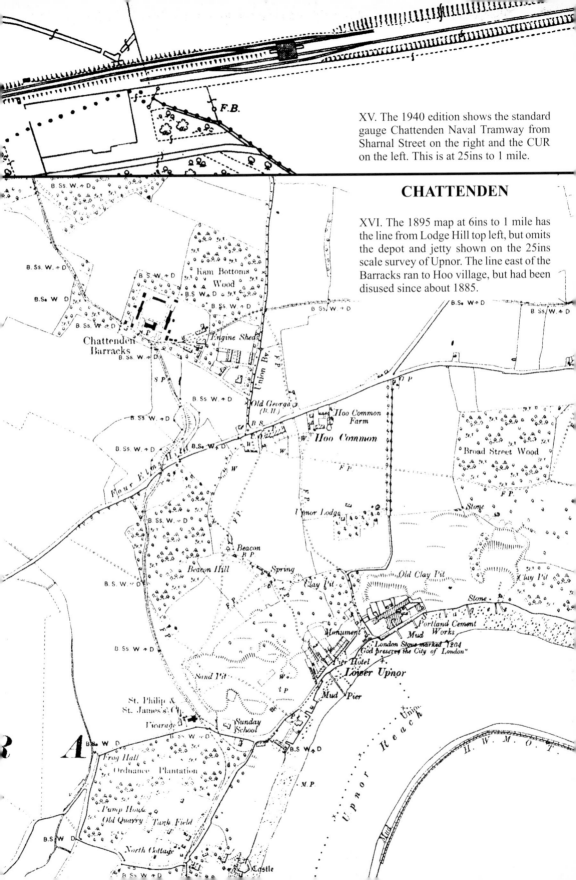

F.B.

XV. The 1940 edition shows the standard gauge Chattenden Naval Tramway from Sharnal Street on the right and the CUR on the left. This is at 25ins to 1 mile.

CHATTENDEN

XVI. The 1895 map at 6ins to 1 mile has the line from Lodge Hill top left, but omits the depot and jetty shown on the 25ins scale survey of Upnor. The line east of the Barracks ran to Hoo village, but had been disused since about 1885.

B Ss. W. ↑ D

B. Ss. W. ↑ D

B. S. W ↑ D

B. S. W. ↑ D

B. S. W. ↑ D

Ram Bottoms Wood

B. S W. ↑ D

B. S. W. ↑ D

B.Ss/W. ↑ D

B.S. W. ↑ D

B Ss W. ↑ D

Chattenden Barracks

Engine Sheds

B. Ss. W. ↑ D

Union By.

S P

B. Ss. W. ↑ D

Old George (P. H.)

B. S.

Hoo Common Farm

B. Ss. W. ↑ D

B.S. W. ↑ D

W

Hoo Common

Broad Street Wood

Four Elm Hill

B. Ss. W. ↑ D

W

F P

F P

Upnor Lodge

Stone

B. Ss. W. ↑ D

Beacon B P

Spring

Old Clay Pit

Clay Pit

Beacon Hill

Clay Pit

B. S. W ↑ D

Clay Pit

Stone

Monument

Portland Cement Mud Works

Sand Pit

"London Stone marked 1204 God preserve the City of London"

B Ss W ↑ D

Pier Hotel

Lower Upnor

St. Philip & St. James's Ch.

Mud Pier

Vicarage

Sunday School

Union Reach

B S W D

B S W ↑ D

B. S W ↑ D

H.W.M.O.T.

Frog Hall

Ordnance Plantation

M. P.

Mud

Pump House

Old Quarry Tank Field

North Cottage

B S W D

Castle

B. S. W ↑ D

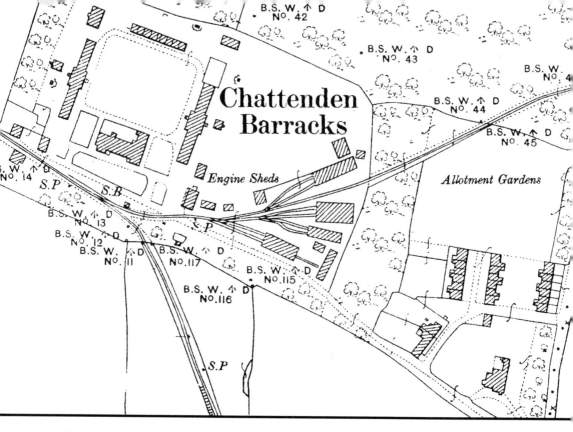

XVII. The 1897 map indicates the extent of the Army accommodation. BSW↑D indicates Boundary Stone War Department. The disused line to Hoo is on the right of this 25ins scale survey.

48. We now have three photographs from 29th July 1950. No. 89 was one of a number of four-wheeled battery electric locomotives from Greenwood & Batley used for shunting ammunition wagons. There were also some by Wingrove & Rogers. (J.H.Moss/R.S.Carpenter coll.)

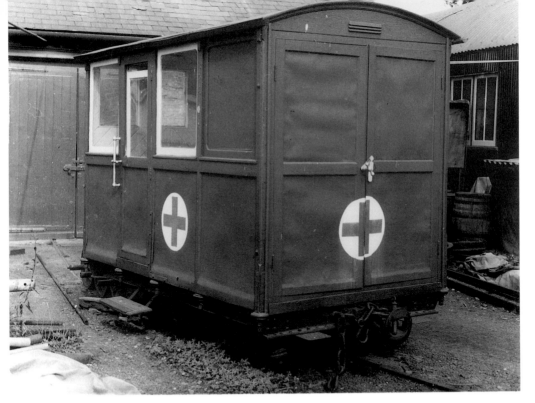

49. Few railways could include an ambulance in its stock list, although the Ffestiniog still includes a hearse. A modern ambulance is included in picture 41. (J.H.Moss/R.S.Carpenter coll.)

50. While the FfR had longitudinal seats on its original coaches, they did have floors. The extended roof was intended to protect the dangling legs of ratings, provided that the rain descended vertically. (J.H.Moss/R.S.Carpenter coll.)

51. Three rolling stock views from August 1954 follow. The hand-wound crane was fitted with clamps to secure it to the rails. (R.M.Casserley)

52. This Emmett-style van had a projection to accommodate the brake handle. It extends beyond the line of its buffer, so two vans could not be coupled together. (R.M.Casserley)

53. No. 42 *Norbury* was an 0-4-2T new from Peckett in 1934. It was scrapped in 1955. Fourteen different steam locomotives had worked on the line. (R.M.Casserley)

54. We can enjoy three general views taken in April 1956 after the arrival of the train seen previously at Lodge Hill. A fire extinguisher, a canal boat chimney and a motor cycle light were seldom chosen to enhance the appearance of a locomotive. (J.J.Smith)

NO EXIT

55. The management found a good use for a coach devoid of a floor - it certainly looked more functional on sleepers, than on bogies. The signal box gives the impression of having been extended. (J.J.Smith)

56. The engine sheds and workshops are seen from the west. The course of the railway northwards was later converted into a road by the MOD. Coaches are standing on the former line to Hoo. (J.J.Smith)

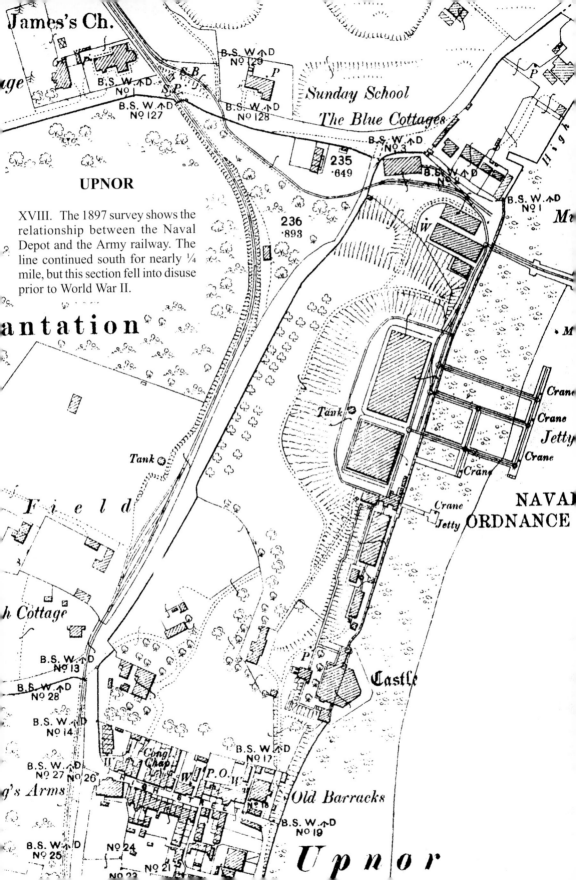

James's Ch.

UPNOR

XVIII. The 1897 survey shows the relationship between the Naval Depot and the Army railway. The line continued south for nearly ¼ mile, but this section fell into disuse prior to World War II.

antation

Sunday School
The Blue Cottages

B.S. W ⋀ D No 129

P

B.S. W ⋀ D No 1

S.B.
S.P.

B.S. W ⋀ D No 127

B.S. W ⋀ D No 128

B.S. W ⋀ D No 3

B.S. W ⋀ D No

235 ·649

B.S. W ⋀ D No 1

236 ·893

W

F i e l d

Tank

Tank

Crane

Crane

Jetty

Crane

Crane

Jetty

Crane

Jetty

NAVAL
ORDNANCE

h Cottage

B.S. W ⋀ D No 13

B.S. W ⋀ D No 28

B.S. W ⋀ D No 14

P

Castle

Cong'l.
Chap.

W

P.O.

B.S. W ⋀ D No 27 No 26

g's Arms

B.S. W ⋀ D No 17

Old Barracks

B.S. W ⋀ D No 25

No 24

No 21

B.S. W ⋀ D No 19

U p n o r

57. The bridge over the A228 Rochester-Grain road is seen from a special train on 7th April 1956. Some of the rolling stock went to the Welshpool & Llanfair Railway, notably Drewry 0-6-0 diesel no. 2263 of 1949. (A.E.Bennett)

58. This is a southward view from a position near the top of the map; the line on the left descends to the jetty. Both sets of level crossing gates and both staff platforms are visible in this 1956 view. (J.J.Smith)

DAVINGTON LIGHT RAILWAY

59. Much of the two mile long metre gauge railway is superimposed on map VIII. It was opened in November 1916 by the Admiralty to serve one of its munition factories. Three trains of four coaches operated ten return trips at each end of every working day. They conveyed about 2500 workers daily, men and women travelling in separate trains. During the day, the line carried mines, bombs, shells and the like to Davington, where they were loaded onto lorries. All traffic ceased after 24 months, following the end of hostilities. Petrol locomotives worked in the factories, but three 0-6-0STs were supplied by Manning Wardle for the main line. They were auctioned after the war and were exported to Brazil, where no. 3 was photographed in December 1988, after withdrawal at Tubarao Works. (M.Shelmerdine)

60. The Davington terminus was partly in a cutting and included an engine shed (right). The transfer siding is in the background, right of centre. (Unknown)

LYDD RANGES

XIX.   The area of the practice ranges is fenced and is strictly out of bounds to the public. The 2ft gauge system has been drawn on the 1940 survey scaled up to 2½ins to 1 mile. Top right is the SR station from which a standard gauge line to the camp was built in 1883 (see *Hastings to Ashford* pictures 79-82). It was lifted in 1927. A loop line was laid on the ranges, but the track was removed by 1934. Narrow gauge lines were laid south of the camp in 1936-40, but there was no connection to the station. There were still 15 route miles in use in 1990, but this had been reduced to five by 2000. The tracks south west of the Camp are known as Holmstone Run and those south thereof as Galloways Run.

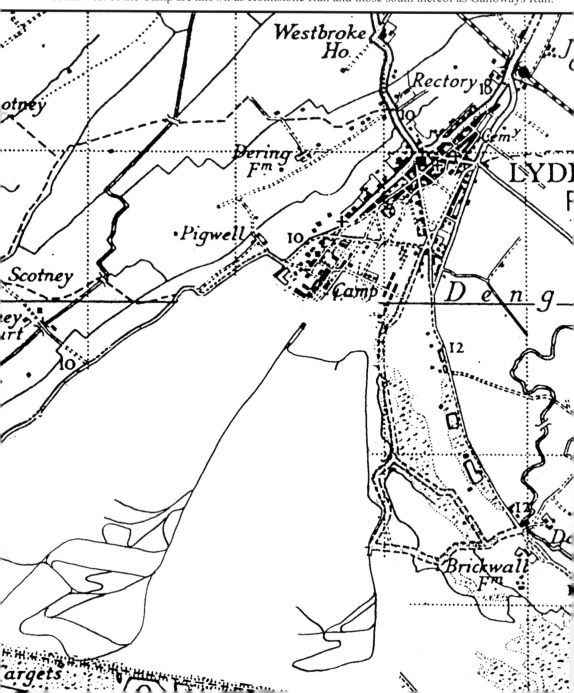

61. Five mobile targets are carried on petrol powered Wickham trolleys, which are capable of 15mph and are speed-controlled by ramps between the rails. The shingle banks protect the tracks and the vehicles. Known as "Jinx", there were over 30 in the 1980s, but, in the early years, wagons bearing targets were simply winched along using long wires. (S.Percival)

62. A 1965 photograph shows Ruston & Hornsby no. 2, one of five from that manufacturer. The coach was provided for the track maintenance gang, which comprised four men in 1990. (C.M.Jackson)

63. An August 1995 panorama includes Dungeness Nuclear Power Station and two of the five Hunslet diesels that now form the fleet. There are eight bogie wagons, eight four-wheelers and an open coach, seen on the left. (C.M.Jackson)

64. The locomotive shed and camp sidings were recorded in 1969. The coach now carries a gas cylinder externally, to supply an interior heater. Note that the entire area is composed of round pebbles, which do not promote track stability. (C.M.Jackson)

3. Pleasure

BREDGAR & WORMSHILL LIGHT RAILWAY

The half-mile long line is a most splendid 2ft gauge eccentricity created by a group of friends in a very beautiful location near these villages, which are situated between Sittingbourne and Hollingbourne. Locomotive restoration started in 1975 and the track has been steadily extended subsequently.

WARREN WOOD

65. Viewed from the headshunt at the west end of the line on 18th August 1999 is no. 4 *Armistice,* which is standing between the engine shed and the turntable. The island platform and signal box are on the left. (V.Mitchell)

66. Standing outside the spacious engine shed in 1998 are (from left to right) no. 4 *Armistice,* a Bagnall 0-4-0ST of 1919; no. 2 *Katie,* an 0-6-0WT built by Arn Jung in 1931 and no. 1 *Bronhilde* an 0-4-0WT from Schwartzkopf in 1929. This was obtained from Bressingham Steam Museum in 1979. All are finished in lined Brunswick green. (BWR)

67. The line's fourth steam locomotive is no. 3 *Harrogate,* an 0-6-0ST built for that town's gasworks by Peckett in 1944. It languished unused on the Ffestiniog Railway from 1957 to 1987, when it was part-exchanged for one of three new Baguley-Drewry diesels. The Ff R named it *Harlech Castle.* The original gaswork's ugly cab was replaced by this conventional one in 1989. (BWR)

68. No. 1 *Bronhilde* nears the end of its journey as it passes between the ornate canopy and the floral displays, all planned to give visual pleasure to the visitor. The coaches have been built on site and styled to be typical of those running on the narrow gauge in Britain in the 1920s, although the seating is more modern. (BWR)

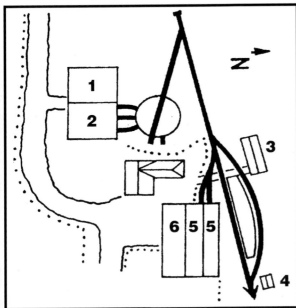

XX. 1999 track layout

1. Shed for non-operational locomotives and other exhibits
2. Running shed for 2ft gauge locomotives
3. Mess room
4. Signal box
5. Carriage sheds
6. Tea room

69. One of the other objectives is to give an impression of the goods carrying capabilities of former narrow gauge railways. Seen here is part of the impressive fleet of wagons; the van at the front is from the Chattenden & Upnor Railway, while other bodies were built in the nearby workshops on regauged Admiralty frames. The signal box has seven levers and other authentic equipment. (BWR)

CHALKHOLE FALL

70. An intermediate halt is provided near a chalk quarry, close to the point at which the line leaves the open paddock area to enter woodland. It is a pleasant place to dwell on an operating day and feast one's eyes on the passing trains. (P.G.Barnes)

71. The main line is on the left in this view towards the terminus, the white platform of which is in the right distance. The sidings in the foreground are for demonstration goods trains and a goods shed base is on the right. The signal box has five levers. (BWR)

72. Nos 1 and 2 pose in the beautiful woodland setting. New rail was purchased in 1997 and the track was relaid to the BWLR's universal high standard, using Pandrol clips as seen. The site is usually strictly private, but educational groups can be accommodated by arrangement. However, there are public open days on the first Sunday of each month from May to September. Telephone 01622 884254 for details. (BWR)

HERNE BAY PIER TRAMWAY

The 3640ft long pier was designed by Thomas Telford and was opened in June 1832. A sail-powered car was introduced on 13th June 1833, it conveying both luggage and passengers on the final part of their journey from London. The population rose from 1876 in 1831 to 3041 in 1841 as a result of the improved transport from the City, but the steamer service ceased in 1862, owing to the competition of the main line railway. The pier was closed in 1864, due to its poor condition, and subsequently demolished.

The second pier was completed in August 1873, but was only 3200ft in length. It was extended to 3920ft between 1896 and 1898, and the 3ft 4½ins construction railway was retained for passengers. It was electrified at 250volts DC, the generator also providing pier lighting. The tramway opened with one car (Brush body on Peckham trucks) on 1st April 1899. Two trailer cars were added in 1901 and a luggage wagon followed. All stock was scrapped during World War I.

A Strode petrol-electric tram arrived in July 1925 for the reopening and a Hibberd battery-electric vehicle followed in 1934. Steamer services ceased for the third time with the advent of World War II in 1939 and the stock was scrapped for the last time after the war.

73. The Strode car was used as a trailer after 1934. The shed beyond it was used for charging the Hibberd tram. The photograph was taken in February 1948. (J.H.Meredith)

74. The only siding was at the landward end and is seen on 22nd September 1948. The active tramway can be seen in the final two pictures in the Middleton Press *North Kent Tramways* album. (J.H.Meredith)

75. The 250yd long 2ft gauge line is on private land and not open to the public. Track laying commenced in 1995, using ex-RHDR rail and ex-BR sleepers, halved. There are three sidings at the end at which the locomotive shed is situated and the stock comprises six wagons, mostly ex-Bretts. One has been adapted to carry passengers and is seen behind Orenstein & Koppel 0-6-0ST *Elsa,* which was built in 1913 and was shipped from Zimbabwe in 1989. It is seen on a temporary line near Canterbury in 1984. (Rev T.Hamer)

MARGATE DREAMLAND MINIATURE RAILWAY

76. The 15ins gauge amusement park oval line opened in 1920, the rolling stock coming from Rhyl. The site was adjacent to Margate Sands (see next map) and there was a single station near Belgrave Road. An end-to-end line was created in 1924. Seen on 6th May 1951 is *Billie,* a 4-4-2 built by Albert Barnes in about 1924 for use at Rhyl. (J.H.Meredith)

77. No. 2 *Prince Edward of Wales* was photographed on 30th August 1953. It was constructed by Bassett-Lowke in 1909 and was named *Red Dragon* when it was running at Rhyl. (J.H.Meredith)

78. Seen on 12th June 1963 is the line's petrol locomotive, which had been built by R.H.Morse in 1939. It had only one bogie and was thus a 4-4-0. The machine had previously run on the Deans Mill Garden Railway at Lindfield in Sussex. (J.H.Meredith)

79. *Billie* had lost a smoke deflector by the time she was photographed on 6th August 1979. At the far end of the three tracks is a locomotive traverser. (P.Groom)

MARGATE PIER RAILWAY

80. The 10¼ins gauge line ran on the jetty or harbour arm from 1948 to 1963, but not a pier in the present sense. The power was provided by this model of the *Flying Scotsman* and one of the Royal Scot class, *Queen of Scots,* constructed in 1947. (J.H.Meredith)

81. *Flying Scotsman* was built for the line by Carland Engineering and was photographed on 12th June 1963, while its boiler was apparently connected to a mains supply. The rail section and sleeper spacing also spoil the effect. A new railway was laid on a timber pier in 1964 and was operated with a model "Western" class diesel, built by Curwen & Newbery. The line was in use until 1975. (J.H.Meredith)

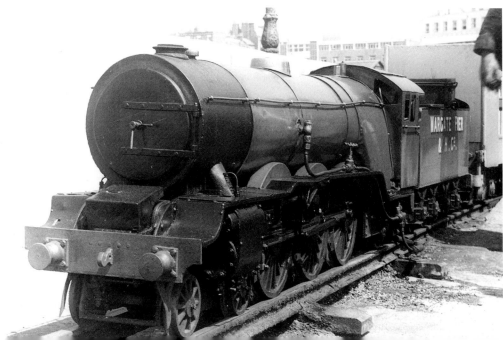

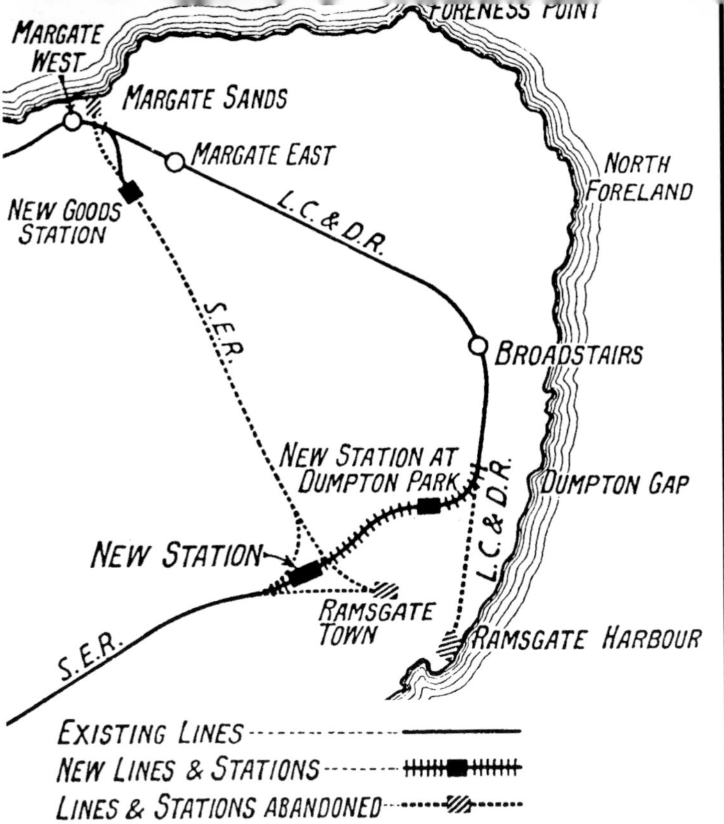
FORENESS POINT
MARGATE WEST
MARGATE SANDS
MARGATE EAST
NORTH FORELAND
NEW GOODS STATION
L.C.&D.R.
S.E.R.
BROADSTAIRS
NEW STATION AT DUMPTON PARK
DUMPTON GAP
L.C.&D.R.
NEW STATION
RAMSGATE TOWN
RAMSGATE HARBOUR
S.E.R.
EXISTING LINES
NEW LINES & STATIONS
LINES & STATIONS ABANDONED

RAMSGATE TUNNEL RAILWAY

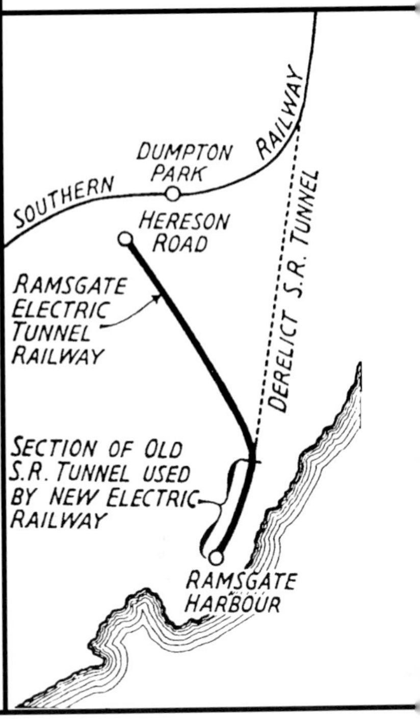
SOUTHERN RAILWAY
DUMPTON PARK
HERESON ROAD
RAMSGATE ELECTRIC TUNNEL RAILWAY
DERELICT S.R. TUNNEL
SECTION OF OLD S.R. TUNNEL USED BY NEW ELECTRIC RAILWAY
RAMSGATE HARBOUR

XXI. The tunnel was built to reach the LCDR terminus, which is illustrated in the photographs 106-113 in our *Sittingbourne to Ramsgate* album. This map shows how Margate Sands and Ramsgate Harbour stations were abandoned in July 1926, following the opening of a short length of new line. (Railway Magazine)

XXII. Only 300yds of the 1863 tunnel was used for the new electric railway; 700yds of new 9ft bore was required, much of it being on a 1 in 15 gradient. The line opened on 31st July 1936 and was laid to two-foot gauge. (Railway Magazine)

RAMSGATE HARBOUR

82. The title on the nameboard was due to the fact that the trains passed tableaux depicting scenes from around the world on the first part of their journey. The sign shows that the railway served other purposes. (R. Shephard)

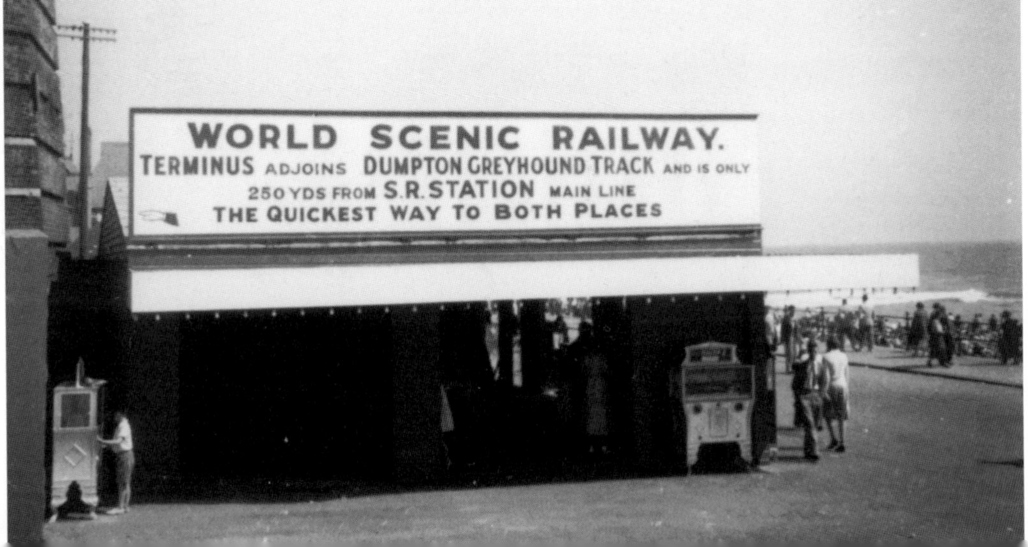
WORLD SCENIC RAILWAY.
TERMINUS ADJOINS DUMPTON GREYHOUND TRACK AND IS ONLY
250 YDS FROM S.R. STATION MAIN LINE
THE QUICKEST WAY TO BOTH PLACES

83. The site of the LCDR terminus had been used for a fairground and part of the tunnel housed lions. These two pre-war photographs illustrate the terminus of the World Scenic Railway in its original form. (R.Shephard)

84. The station had changed completely when recorded in June 1963; compare this with picture no. 83. Operation ceased on 26th September 1965, following a runaway on 1st July, but some of the coaches are still in use at the Hollycombe Steam Collection in Hampshire. (J.H.Meredith)

HERESON ROAD

85. The upper terminus comprised three wooden platforms for two tracks. A train could be unloaded from one side, while passengers joined from the other. The line was closed from September 1939 to May 1946.
(J.H.Meredith)

86. Both the old and new tunnels were transformed into air raid shelters for 60,000 people. A further three miles of tunnels were bored and 18 entrances were provided.
(Railway Magazine)

87. The terminus was photographed on 5th July 1953, by which time the platforms had been rebuilt in concrete. The two power units came from English Electric and were supplied with current at 460 volts DC.
(J.H.Meredith)

SITTINGBOURNE & KEMSLEY
LIGHT RAILWAY

As mentioned in the section on Bowaters, about two miles of their railway was leased to the LCGB, which adopted the title above although it was not a Light Railway within the scope of the 1896 Act. An independent operating company was established on 1st January 1972. The first train, for members only, ran on Good Friday of 1970 and the line opened to the public on the following day, 28th March. It is now marketed as "Sittingbourne's Steam Railway" and operates four to seven return journeys at weekends, and on some other days, from Easter to October, plus Christmas. The talking timetable is on 01795 424899.

SITTINGBOURNE VIADUCT

88. Two photographs from 18th June 1978 emphasise the industrial nature of the environs. There are few locations where former industrial locomotives can be seen working in their natural habitat. The 1905 Kerr Stuart 0-4-2ST *Premier* stands under the piping gantry and alongside the platform and teashop. (T.Heavyside)

89. *Premier* is approaching the southern terminus with four ex-Bowater coaches. The line has ten bogie coaches; four of them are ex-CUR. The concrete viaduct is about ½ mile long and was closed on safety grounds from 20th December 1992 until 21st April 1996. The suffix "Viaduct" was added to the station name in 1998. (T.Heavyside)

MILTON REGIS HALT

90. During the viaduct closure period, trains terminated at an ash platform in a desolate location, the nearest public amenity being a rubbish tip. A short siding was laid to accommodate a mobile booking office/waiting room and a diesel locomotive, used for shunting the train back after arrival, to release the steam engine. This northward view is from 10th April 1993 and includes *Triumph* with ex-CUR coaches. A new permanent platform, on the other side of the track, was opened on 2nd April 2000. (V.Mitchell)

KEMSLEY DOWN

91. The approach is seen from the north in August 1992, along with the well insulated pipes of the mills and an ex-SR signal post. There is no public access to this station, other than by train. The pipes convey steam from Kemsley Mill and return condensate and effluent. The signals control arrivals and departures. (P.G.Barnes)

92.   Initially, the SKLR used Bowater's shed at Sittingbourne, but this permanent depot was established at the other end of the line in August 1971. *Triumph* is seen outside the shed on 29th August 1992. The mailbag apparatus on the left has moved to a more appropriate home. (P.G.Barnes)

93. Turning to the north, we see *Superb* (left) and *Triumph* at the platform on 7th October 1989. The headboard is the one seen earlier (picture no. 24); the line had been preserved for 20 years by that time. The narrow gauge fleet comprises seven steam and two diesel locomotives, but not all are in working order. (J.H.Meredith)

4. Main Line
ROMNEY HYTHE & DYMCHURCH RAILWAY

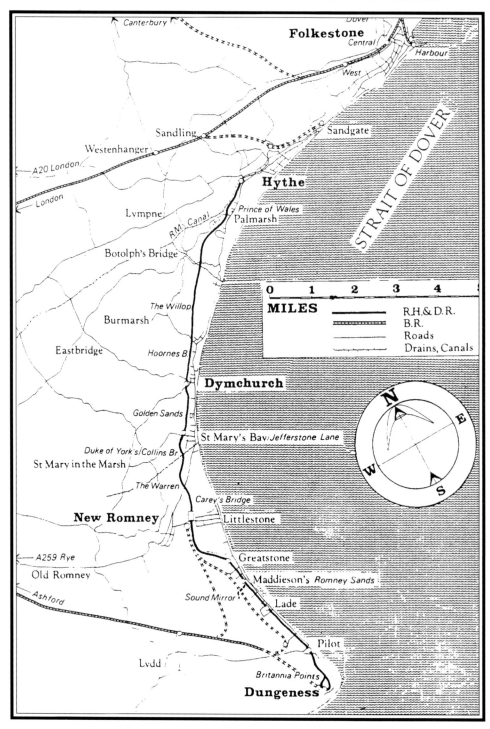

This 15ins gauge line was unusual amongst narrow gauge railways in having been opened with double track throughout. Its main purpose was to provide an interesting occupation for its millionaire owner, Captain J.E.P.Howey, who had been "bitten by the 15-inch bug" in 1911 and now wanted something bigger and better than his previous garden railway, with miniature versions of main line locomotives and fast running. Its secondary purpose was to provide a means of transport between the places of its title and to facilitate the development of the coastal areas between them, principally for holiday use. Traffic began on 16th July 1927 and a regular service was offered throughout the year. For these reasons, we use the term "main line" for this most remarkable railway.

The terminus at New Romney soon had to be altered to allow the double track to be extended to Dungeness in two stages in 1928, but this section had only a limited Winter service. The railway was under military control from 1940 to 1945 and reopened in stages in 1946-47. Since that time, the route south of New Romney has been single track and very few public trains have run in Winter at all.

The popular change to holidays abroad hit the line badly, but it survived to continue to offer the sight of former main line practice in miniature. Most of the infrastructure was life expired by the late 1960s and truncation of the route was considered. Instead, a long term restoration programme was devised and this was overseen by John B. Snell, who was managing director from 1972 to the end of the century. The line is extensively illustrated in our *Romneyrail* album; herein we have tried to include unpublished views from fresh viewpoints.

XXIII. The 1981 map includes Greatstone, Lade and Pilot, although these stations closed in 1977. Maddieson's Camp was renamed Romney Sands in April 1981 and St. Mary's Bay became Jefferstone Lane at the same time. (J.B.Snell)

HYTHE

94. A westward view from about 1937 includes evidence of the 1933 extension to the roof, which protected passengers on all four platforms. Seldom photographed from this angle is the carriage siding, which was slightly raised to facilitate axlebox examination and lubrication. On the left is part of the ramp which carried ballast wagons prior to their discharge. This traffic ceased here in 1948. (RHDRAA/J.Wootton)

95. This location is near the right border of the previous photograph, but was pictured on 22nd September 1968 as no. 1 *Green Goddess* took water from the infrequently used tank. The line from the curved rails gave direct access to the turntable until 1974, when the car park was extended up to the station roof. (A.G.Wells)

96. No. 7 *Typhoon* was recorded prior to departure with the first morning train on 27th September 1987. The original 30ft turntable had been replaced by this 40ft model in 1951. The engine shed was leased out to a manufacturer of miniature locomotives. The signal box contained a 16-lever frame, which was fully interlocked. (P.Groom)

DYMCHURCH

97. No. 3 *Southern Maid* stands devoid of nameplates in mid-1927, while a passenger ignores the order on the footbridge. Initially 60 of these uncomfortable and unsatisfactory four-wheeled coaches were built. They were followed by a further 55, but were all short lived. The two batches had different board widths, as is evident here. (A.G.Nash coll.)

ST. MARY'S BAY

98. There was no access for lorries to the workshops at New Romney and so the level crossing here was a convenient place to erect a hoist to transfer the boilers of *Green Goddess* and *Hurricane* in October 1955. They were later found to be beyond repair. (RHDRAA/G.Barlow)

NEW ROMNEY

99. No. 2 *Northern Chief* is at the arrival platform of the terminus soon after its opening. We view it from the departure platform and look across the carriage siding and engine release road. (RHDRAA/ N.Danger coll.)

100. The station and trackwork underwent several major alterations. The first was in preparation for the opening to Dungeness, when an up through platform was provided south of the station (and road). It was in the position seen from 1931-1973. In the background are the workshops (left) and the running shed (right). No. 3 *Southern Maid* is running in from Hythe in the late 1950s. (K.G.Harvie)

101. A southward view in April 1947 has the through lines on the right, one station clock tower, two carriage sheds and three semaphore signals. A footbridge was erected close to the nearest signal in about 1951. (H.C.Casserley)

102. The extension to Dungeness necessitated the provision of two tunnels under the road, but as they were prone to flooding, their floors were raised, reducing the headroom to 5ft 9ins. Beyond *Northern Chief* on 5th July 1958 is a colour light signal; this type was used universally at the station from 1962 until 1991. The mile post on the right was originally zero, but was changed to 8¼ - from Hythe. (RHDRAA/N.Danger coll.)

103. This May 1962 view reveals how much lower the Dungeness lines were than the terminal ones. No. 6 *Samson* is at platform 3; access to platform 4 was via the footbridge. The level crossing gate in the background is for the standard gauge line from the BR station to the RHDR yard on the right. (J.H.Meredith)

ROMNEY HYTHE & DYMCHURCH RLY.

HYTHE to

BURMARSH ROAD

(DYMCHURCH)

(Passenger Ticket Only)

SINGLE FARE

See conditions on back

2495

Romney Hythe & Dymchurch Rly

Hythe to

BURMARSH ROAD

(Dymchurch)

(Passenger Ticket Only)

SINGLE FARE

See Conditions on back.

10355

104. Major improvements are seen in progress on 29th May 1974, as the biggest narrow gauge train shed in Britain was nearing completion and some passengers make an unorthodox entry. All the platforms would henceforth be on the same level. (J.H.Meredith)

105. The new shed covered not only all four platforms, but four carriage sidings as well. Since the introduction of school trains in 1977, the station is closed for only a few weeks each year. Works trains can be seen at the less busy times. This one was recorded early on 7th Sepember 1980, the locomotive being no. PW2. (P.Groom)

106. The footbridge was moved from the Hythe end of the station to this position in 1966 and is seen from the footplate of no. 5 *Hercules* on 27th August 1981. This was one of two 4-8-2s built by Davey Paxman in 1926 with the stone traffic in mind. The other was no. 6 *Samson*. (P.Groom)

107. The RHDR purchased seven 4-6-2s for passenger services between 1925 and 1931. To assist in the construction work, it obtained 0-4-0 no. 4 *The Bug* from Krauss in Germany. After a long period in a scrapyard in Belfast, it was restored and was photographed at the May Gala in 1988. (P.Groom)

ROMNEY HYTHE & DYMCHURCH RLY

DOG TICKET

Zone Fare   15 Miles

(Accompanied by passenger)

SINGLE FARE

Conditions on back

2012

108. One of the other notable improvements in the Snell era was the provision of an electrically operated turntable. It was installed in 1987 on part of the site of the original terminus. No. 3 *Southern Maid* was recorded on it on 5th March 1988. The previous turntable and the signal box can be glimpsed in picture 117. (P.Groom)

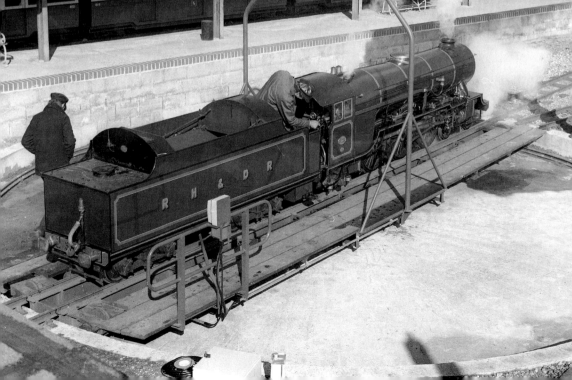

GREATSTONE

109. A 1955 photograph features the redundant signal box to which a shelter had been attached. Both stood for about another ten years. There has been some doubt whether the box ever functioned; however, the signals were installed and were photographed in use. (RHDRAA/A.G.Wells)

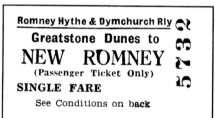

Romney Hythe & Dymchurch Rly
Greatstone Dunes to
NEW ROMNEY
(Passenger Ticket Only)
SINGLE FARE
See Conditions on back

5732

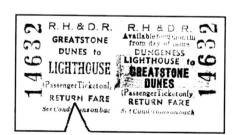

R. H. & D. R.   R. H. & D. R.
GREATSTONE   Available for 2 month
DUNES to   from day of issue
                        DUNGENESS
LIGHTHOUSE   LIGHTHOUSE to
                        GREATSTONE
(Passenger Ticket onl,   DUNES
RETURN FARE   (Passenger Ticket only,
See Cond ons on bac   RETURN FARE
                        See Conditions on back

14632   14632

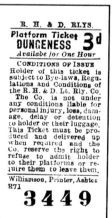

R. H. & D. RLYS.
Platform Ticket
DUNGENESS **3**d
Availabe for One Hour

CONDITIONS OF ISSUE
Holder of this ticket is
subject to Bye-laws, Regu-
lations and Conditions of
the R. H. & D. Lt. Rly. Co.
The Co. is not under
any conditions liable for
personal injury, loss, dam-
age, delay or detention
to holder or their luggage.
This Ticket must be pro-
duced and delivered up
when required and the
Co. reserve the right to
refuse to admit holder
to their platforms or re-
quire them to leave them.

Williamson, Printer, Ashton
R71

3449

PILOT

110. A temporary terminus north of the later station was in use from May to August in 1928. The locomotive is about to return to Hythe, having used the turning triangle, part of which is visible between the third and fourth telephone poles. The area is now covered by dwellings. (RHDRAA/N.Danger coll.)

DUNGENESS

111. The permanent terminus was built on an equally desolate area of windswept shingle, all of which belonged to the Southern Railway. The railway ends with a long loop, which eliminates the turning problem. From left to right in this 1953 panorama are the RHDR ticket office (the refreshment room is behind it), the ex-SR station (disused since 1937) and the toilet block (with water tank above and windpump beyond). This building had earlier been used as a signal box. One of the two 1934 luggage vans is at the rear of the train. (RHDRAA/N.Danger coll.)

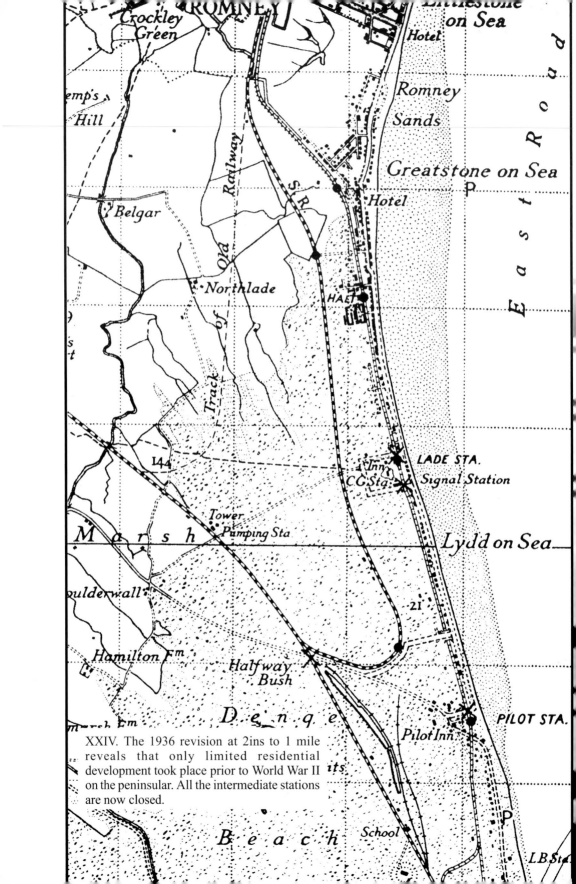

ROMNEY

Littlestone
on Sea

Crockley
Green

Hotel

Romney

emp's
Hill

Sands

S.R.

Greatstone on Sea

Railway

P

Belgar

Hotel

Northlade

Old

HALT

of

Track

144

LADE STA.

Inn

CG Sta.

Signal Station

Tower
Pumping Sta

M a r s h

Lydd on Sea

oulderwall

21

Hamilton Fm

Halfway
Bush

D e n g e

PILOT STA.

rsh Fm

Pilot Inn

XXIV. The 1936 revision at 2ins to 1 mile
reveals that only limited residential
development took place prior to World War II
on the peninsular. All the intermediate stations
are now closed.

its

P

School

B e a c h

L.B.Sta.

East Road

ROLLING STOCK

112. An unusual use of the term rolling stock was recorded on 19th March 1954, as the frame of *Southern Maid* was rotated following overhaul. Note the hand operated tackle and the now-banned asbestos lagging. (RHDRAA/G.A.Barlow)

113. A rare meaning of "rolling stock" was demonstrated on 3rd May 1954, when no. 5 *Hercules* turned on its side between New Romney and Greatstone due to the effect of a gale on the leading vehicle. This was a four-wheeled semi-open coach with guards compartment, known as a "Jumping Jack". All four of these post-war vehicles were withdrawn immediately. (RHDRAA/G.A.Barlow)

114. Most of the early locomotives have been seen, except this unique machine created from a 1914 Rolls Royce Silver Ghost in 1932. It operated most Winter trains from 1933 to 1940 and is shown in other guises in the introduction to our *Romneyrail* volume. This is its form in about 1938. (RHDRAA/N.Danger coll.)

115. Rarely photographed are some of the wooden-bodied wagons used during the construction of the line. They are seen in one of the terminal platforms at New Romney in September 1967. (RHDRAA/A.G.Wells)

116. Many coach bodies were destroyed during World War II and so the stock of the Eaton Hall Railway was purchased in 1947. It included this 16-seater from 1904 and a bogie van of similar age. They are seen at Dymchurch on 22nd July 1947, after being cut down to fit the tunnels at New Romney. (RHDRAA)

117. Featured on the left are two of six bogie ballast wagons purchased from the Ravenglass & Eskdale Railway in 1929. They conveyed crushed stone from Dungeness until 1940, when two were fitted with guns and armour plate. One was destroyed and the frames of the others were fitted with various coach bodies in 1947. (RHDRAA/N.Danger coll.)

118. Two of the five surviving ballast wagon frames were fitted with observation saloons, but most of the seats faced inwards. Seen in 1947, one was always included in "The Bluecoaster Limited", a non-stop train introduced that year. The bodies lasted until 1954.
(RHDRAA/J.C.Flemons)

119. There were 63 passenger vehicles in 1999 and 79 (officially) in 1967 when this photograph was taken at New Romney. Nearest are recent rebuilds of 1934 saloons, mostly fitted with sliding doors although one of the awkward inward opening doors can be seen.
(RHDRAA/A.G.Wells)

More illustrations of the railway and its stock can be found in *Romneyrail* (Middleton Press)

R. H. & D. R.
3666 Dungeness Lighthouse to **St. Mary's Bay** (Passenger Ticket Only) Return Fare
See conditions on back.

R. H. & D. R.
Available for 2 months from day of issue
St. Mary's Bay to Dungeness Lighthouse (Passenger Ticket Only) Return Fare **3666**
See conditions on back

ROMNEY HYTHE & DYMCHURCH RLY.
NEW ROMNEY to
Dungeness Lighthouse
(Passenger Ticket Only)
SINGLE FARE
See conditions on back
6784

120. Seen near some of the electro-mechanical signals at New Romney in March 1997 is the ultimate in 15ins gauge luxury. Known as the "Bar Car", this splendid 32-foot long coach carries 16 passengers, in addition to their catering attendant. This magnificent railway deserves all the promotion it can be given. Telephone 01797 362353 for leaflets to distribute and do ride on it! (P.Groom)

MP Middleton Press

Easebourne Lane, Midhurst, W Sussex. GU29 9AZ Tel: 01730 813169 Fax: 01730 812601
If books are not available from your local transport stockist, order direct with cheque,
Visa or Mastercard, post free UK.

BRANCH LINES
Branch Line to Allhallows
Branch Line to Alton
Branch Lines around Ascot
Branch Line to Ashburton
Branch Lines around Bodmin
Branch Line to Bude
Branch Lines around Canterbury
Branch Lines around Chard & Yeovil
Branch Lines around Cromer
Branch Lines of East London
Branch Lines to Effingham Junction
Branch Lines around Exmouth
Branch Line to Fairford
Branch Lines around Gosport
Branch Line to Hawkhurst
Branch Line to Hayling
Branch Lines to Horsham
Branch Lines around Huntingdon
Branch Line to Kingswear
Branch Lines to Launceston & Princetown
Branch Lines to Longmoor
Branch Line to Looe
Branch Line to Lyme Regis
Branch Lines around March
Branch Lines around Midhurst
Branch Line to Minehead
Branch Line to Moretonhampstead
Branch Lines to Newport (IOW)
Branch Line to Padstow
Branch Lines around Plymouth
Branch Lines to Seaton and Sidmouth
Branch Line to Selsey
Branch Lines around Sheerness
Branch Line to Shrewsbury
Branch Line to Swanage *updated*
Branch Line to Tenterden
Branch Lines to Torrington
Branch Lines to Tunbridge Wells
Branch Line to Upwell
Branch Lines around Weymouth
Branch Lines around Wimborne
Branch Lines around Wisbech

NARROW GAUGE BRANCH LINES
Branch Line to Lynton
Branch Lines around Portmadoc 1923-46
Branch Lines around Porthmadog 1954-94
Branch Line to Southwold
Two-Foot Gauge Survivors
Romneyrail
Vivarais Narrow Gauge

SOUTH COAST RAILWAYS
Ashford to Dover
Bournemouth to Weymouth
Brighton to Eastbourne
Brighton to Worthing
Dover to Ramsgate
Eastbourne to Hastings
Hastings to Ashford
Portsmouth to Southampton
Southampton to Bournemouth
Worthing to Chichester

SOUTHERN MAIN LINES
Basingstoke to Salisbury
Bromley South to Rochester
Crawley to Littlehampton
Dartford to Sittingbourne
East Croydon to Three Bridges
Epsom to Horsham
Exeter to Barnstaple

Exeter to Tavistock
Faversham to Dover
London Bridge to East Croydon
Orpington to Tonbridge
Tonbridge to Hastings
Salisbury to Yeovil
Swanley to Ashford
Tavistock to Plymouth
Victoria to East Croydon
Waterloo to Windsor
Waterloo to Woking
Woking to Portsmouth
Woking to Southampton
Yeovil to Exeter

EASTERN MAIN LINES
Fenchurch Street to Barking
Ipswich to Saxmundham
Liverpool Street to Ilford

WESTERN MAIN LINES
Ealing to Slough
Paddington to Ealing

COUNTRY RAILWAY ROUTES
Andover to Southampton
Bath Green Park to Bristol
Bath to Evercreech Junction
Bournemouth to Evercreech Jn.
Cheltenham to Andover
Croydon to East Grinstead
Didcot to Winchester
East Kent Light Railway
Fareham to Salisbury
Frome to Bristol
Guildford to Redhill
Porthmadog to Blaenau
Reading to Basingstoke
Reading to Guildford
Redhill to Ashford
Salisbury to Westbury
Stratford upon Avon to Cheltenham
Strood to Paddock Wood
Taunton to Barnstaple
Wenford Bridge to Fowey
Westbury to Bath
Woking to Alton
Yeovil to Dorchester

GREAT RAILWAY ERAS
Ashford from Steam to Eurostar
Clapham Junction 50 years of change
Festiniog in the Fifties
Festiniog in the Sixties
Isle of Wight Lines 50 years of change
Railways to Victory 1944-46
SECR Centenary album
Talyllyn 50 years of change
Yeovil 50 years of change

LONDON SUBURBAN RAILWAYS
Caterham and Tattenham Corner
Charing Cross to Dartford
Clapham Jn. to Beckenham Jn.
East London Line
Finsbury Park to Alexandra Palace
Kingston and Hounslow Loops
Lewisham to Dartford
Lines around Wimbledon
London Bridge to Addiscombe
Mitcham Junction Lines
North London Line
South London Line
West Croydon to Epsom

West London Line
Willesden Junction to Richmond
Wimbledon to Epsom

STEAMING THROUGH
Steaming through Cornwall
Steaming through Kent
Steaming through West Hants
Steaming through West Sussex

TRAMWAY CLASSICS
Aldgate & Stepney Tramways
Barnet & Finchley Tramways
Bath Tramways
Bournemouth & Poole Tramways
Brighton's Tramways
Camberwell & W.Norwood Tramways
Clapham & Streatham Tramways
Dover's Tramways
East Ham & West Ham Tramways
Edgware and Willesden Tramways
Eltham & Woolwich Tramways
Embankment & Waterloo Tramways
Enfield & Wood Green Tramways
Exeter & Taunton Tramways
Gosport & Horndean Tramways
Greenwich & Dartford Tramways
Hammersmith & Hounslow Tramways
Hampstead & Highgate Tramways
Hastings Tramways
Holborn & Finsbury Tramways
Ilford & Barking Tramways
Kingston & Wimbledon Tramways
Lewisham & Catford Tramways
Liverpool Tramways 1. Eastern Routes
Liverpool Tramways 2. Southern Routes
Maidstone & Chatham Tramways
North Kent Tramways
Norwich Tramways
Portsmouth's Tramways
Reading Tramways
Seaton & Eastbourne Tramways
Shepherds Bush & Uxbridge Tramways
Southampton Tramways
Southend-on-sea Tramways
Southwark & Deptford Tramways
Stamford Hill Tramways
Twickenham & Kingston Tramways
Victoria & Lambeth Tramways
Waltham Cross & Edmonton Tramways
Walthamstow & Leyton Tramways
Wandsworth & Battersea Tramways

TROLLEYBUS CLASSICS
Croydon Trolleybuses
Bournemouth Trolleybuses
Hastings Trolleybuses
Maidstone Trolleybuses
Reading Trolleybuses
Woolwich & Dartford Trolleybuses

WATERWAY ALBUMS
Kent and East Sussex Waterways
London to Portsmouth Waterway
West Sussex Waterways

MILITARY BOOKS
Battle over Portsmouth
Battle over Sussex 1940
Blitz over Sussex 1941-42
Bombers over Sussex 1943-45
Bognor at War
Military Defence of West Sussex
Secret Sussex Resistance
Sussex Home Guard

OTHER RAILWAY BOOKS
Garraway Father & Son
Index to all Middleton Press stations
Industrial Railways of the South-East
South Eastern & Chatham Railways
London Chatham & Dover Railway
War on the Line (SR 1939-45)